INSIDE THE
JOURNEY
TO A BRAND
NEW ME

Antuan Russ

INSIDE THE
JOURNEY
TO A BRAND
NEW ME

Cover photo: Sonya Russ Photography
Book Cover Design: Gorilla Ink Design House
Editor: Noel Estabrook

ISBN 0-692-52657-9
ISBN 13: 978-0-692-52657-6
Printed in the U.S.A.
Innisfree Publishing Company, LLC
innisfreepublishingcompany@gmail.com

Acknowledgements

"I'm going to write a book."

With that statement, I began down the path of writing a book. Those words would've remained an empty statement, void of meaning, without the assistance of some wonderful people.

Mom, thank you for giving me the appreciation for writing. I'm grateful for your willingness to read and proofread and reread the words in this book.

Dad, without your encouragement and support, this book wouldn't have happened. Whenever I was stuck or felt like quitting, you would ask how the book was going and I'd get back on track.

Bishop Jackson, the timing of our meeting was Divine to say the least. Without your knowledge and willingness to share, this book would be a dream deferred.

Noel Estabrook, your editing prowess tremendously enhanced me as a writer. Your insight was invaluable.

LaRon Stewart, you took my abstract ideas and created an ice cold book cover. You have a gift!

Sonya Russ, so much to thank you for; but for the purpose of this page, I'll keep it brief. Thank you for allowing me the time to write this. Much of this was written between 10:00 PM and 2:00 AM (Dream chaser hours!) And for the wonderful cover photo, I again say thank you! You're ridiculously talented!

To everyone who gave a kind and encouraging word when I told them I was writing a book, thank you! The positive words were well-received. You made me feel that writing a book wasn't just a crazy idea but a very tangible thing.

To those who are in pursuit of their dreams, I dedicate this book. Keep chasing your dreams and enjoy the journey. The world awaits your greatness. The story that follows is proof that you can accomplish anything you want if you refuse to quit.

Preface

For all of my adult life, weight has been a constant issue. This battle was long, grueling, and never-ending. For the longest time, my fight was an exercise in frustration. Pounds would be lost only to be found a few short months later. But not only did the pounds find their way back to my body, they always brought a few extra pounds with them. Each time I lost weight, I managed to regain more weight than I lost. With each failed attempt to gain control of my health, my hope for a life full of adventure and promise slowly dissipated.

I don't know exactly when I decided to raise the white flag of surrender and retreat from the battle but I know I did. I settled into a life ravaged by decisions that directly opposed healthy living. Without hope, I took the "out of sight, out of mind" approach. Sadly, years passed and I successfully ignored my health.

When I finally took an earnest and honest look at my challenges, I discovered that not only was my weight a constant issue during my adult life, but went as far back as to when I was a ten-year-old boy.

The initial meeting with my weight issues began rather innocently in an elementary school classroom. That first meeting has never been forgotten. Even when I thought that day was a distant and faded memory, the ease with which my mind recalled it reminded me that that day was always in the forefront of my thoughts. Regardless of the number of times I pushed that day to the recesses of my mind, it found its way back.

"Take one and pass it down," my teacher instructed. I grabbed the stack of mustard yellow papers from my teacher and placed one on my desk before I gave the remainder of the stack to my friend who was sitting directly behind me. Immediately, the bold dark block letters and pictures caught my attention. The word "football" leaped off the page directly in front of my eyes. Up until this time, the only football experience I had was during recess or after school in the neighborhood. I knew I wanted to play. Before I realized it, my mind drifted to the pageantry of Friday night high school football as I imagined being part of the team. The excitement swelled and thoughts of racing onto the football field as the band played the fight song filled my head!

One of my fondest memories as a child had always been going to high school football games on Friday nights. The anticipation would build throughout the day as the clock sped towards seven o'clock. I would gather my things and rush out of the door as soon as I heard the beginning sounds of the final bell. With all the speed my young body could muster, I would run across the empty grassy field to the high school. Sometimes I was able to catch a glimpse of the group of guys all clad in red and white jerseys.

My mother was a teacher there and, as a result of that, I had access to some of the players. They would give me high fives and make me feel like the coolest elementary school kid ever. Those moments created in me the desire to wear that red and white jersey on Friday nights.

Ironically, the same mustard yellow paper that provided fuel for the dreams of a ten-year-old boy also informally introduced him to the concept of being overweight. At the bottom of the page, the age and weight requirements were printed.

I soon found out that I exceeded the weight limit to play recreation football. Being unable to really grasp why I couldn't play, I simply dismissed the idea. The sting from that day was short-lived but was my first real memory of being overweight. Our encounter was brief and I had no idea how many times our paths would cross as I grew and marched toward adulthood.

After our introduction, my weight issue and I barely spoke. There would be moments where I was forced to acknowledge its existence. Those "pleasantries" would be exchanged as briefly as possible and forgotten with equal speed. As the days passed and the path of my life unfolded, our exchanges became more frequent.

By the time I found myself at my weight loss crossroads, I had given up on the idea of ever being healthy and fit. Muscles and a six pack of abs would never be in my possession. Interestingly enough, in the midst of all the helplessness, the flame of hope was never completely extinguished. There were times where the flame was nothing but a dim flicker; yet it never succumbed to my mindset concerning my health and wellness. That flame fought to stay relevant in my life and every now and then the flicker would grow into a slightly larger flame.

When the flicker did grow, I would attempt to tackle my weight issue once more. Within a few fleeting days, I would lose yet another round in this battle for my health, the flame would return to a dim flicker and the thought of "this is just how it's going to be" would spread its roots further into the soil of my subconscious. As they continued to spread deeper into the terrain of my mind, little by little I abandoned the desire for normalcy. I loosened the grip I had on the idea of shopping in stores without the title 'Big and Tall' in them, the idea of having an active lifestyle, and the idea of life without guilt or shame.

That pattern was repeated numerous times throughout my life. However, all those moments, all those failed attempts, all those times of giving up were not in vain. They led me to a fall day in Greenville, South Carolina a few years ago. It was on that fall day that I decided to get healthy once and for all and so began the journey of a lifetime – the journey to a brand new me.

Chapter One

Defining Moments

Every adversity, every failure, every heartache carries with it the seed of an equal or greater benefit.
– Napoleon Hill

When I look at the origin of my weight loss, I can trace it back to a particular moment in time. As is true of many defining moments, it occurred at a low point in my life which, ironically, I didn't recognize until after it had passed. It arrived on a picturesque autumn day that started no differently than countless other days that had come before. In fact, the only difference with this day was that I was for some reason incapable of ignoring my emotions. Prior to this particular day, I had always possessed an amazing ability to lock my emotions in a box when dealing with people. By doing so, I was able to successfully play whatever role I needed to on the grand stage of life. In retrospect, I now realize this ability was nothing more than a futile attempt at self-preservation.

I was living a life of quiet desperation, only this time my emotions would not cooperate. They refused to stay in their box. For now, every time I found myself in front of a mirror, my emotions jumped out of their prison cell, protesting the sentence of solitary confinement they had been given. For whatever reason, maybe it was fate, on that fall day I was unable to ignore my emotions. I was no longer able to play the happy character as I had done countless times before.

It was a day of celebration. I took the day off work to spend quality time with my wife on her birthday. We had a great time meandering through the perfect fall day, enjoying each other's company. The weather was absolutely amazing, with whimsical white clouds scattered throughout the blue sky and leaves with lively hues of red, orange, and other fall colors providing a pleasant backdrop for our quaint city. I could not have asked for a better day. My wife and I made our way downtown where restaurants, retail stores, and various knick knack shops lined both sides of the street. This was not the downtown of some sprawling metropolis, but one of charm and warmth, perfect for couples who wanted to slowly walk hand in hand laughing with each other. The hustle and bustle common to most cities was replaced with a leisurely pace and trees that dotted the sidewalks and invited you to stop and soak in the scenery.

We made our way to our special spot - the very place where I proposed to her a handful of years ago. There I was with my wife's hand in mine standing on a masterfully crafted suspension bridge overlooking a waterfall just below us. The sound of rushing water and people walking around living life provided a fitting soundtrack for our conversation. We talked, laughed, and enjoyed ourselves as if we were the only two people in the world. It was a moment to relish my wife's laugh, being that it was one of the sounds I enjoyed hearing the most.

As our day wound down, we gathered our belongings and climbed the steps carved out of stone back to the park entrance. My wife took my hand at the top of the steps and told me how wonderful the day had been.

It was then that my defining, life-changing moment began. On the outside, I was smiling. On the inside, however, there was nothing to smile about. I was winded, my knees were aching, my back hurt from walking and climbing the steps. I felt miserable.

"How could this be?" I asked myself. I was still so young. There was no reason I should be physically this far gone. As I conversed with my wife, I was having an internal conversation with myself at the same time.

"You can't keep going like this Antuan, you'll be dead by 40. You're going to need new knees soon. You'll die on the operating table because of your weight, you know obesity and anesthesia don't mix. Look at her. If you don't change something soon, this beautiful young woman is going to be a widow." So on this day meant to celebrate life, I was doing all I could to stop tears from rolling down my cheeks in anguish.

Among all the despair, grief, sadness, guilt, and shame I felt this day, opportunity had also quietly and subtly joined. Opportunity rarely makes a grand entrance. In fact, it usually goes unnoticed. I recognized its presence and I knew I had to take advantage of it. It was a matter of life or death, and it was in that moment that I simply grew sick and tired of being sick and tired. That moment started me on a journey of discovery, struggles, and victories.

I knew something had to change. It was time. To be honest, it was past time. This was not how I envisioned my life. Being held captive by weight was not in the plan. I had been at this point before, but now something was different. There was a sense of urgency that wasn't present before. It was time to face this issue head on. More importantly, it was time to conquer my weight once and for all. How would I do it? What action could I take? When would I start? Later that night, I pondered those questions as I replayed the day's events over and over in my mind like a news reel. As I watched, I was at a complete loss of words for the few fleeting moments that seemed like an eternity.

Just as I was getting over the day's emotional earthquake, the wave of aftershocks and tremors came. I had the proverbial "last straw" moment. I saw a picture taken earlier that day and did not recognize myself. Surely that was not me! Surely that mountain of a man had to be someone else. The man in the picture was smiling but the one looking at the picture was crying inside. I absolutely did not like who I had become.

While looking at the picture, I decided to draw a "line in the sand." It was time for me to go toe to toe with the beast of obesity. This monster was a familiar opponent. We had gone a few rounds before, and he had withstood my early onslaught. He waited me out, knowing that eventually I would lose motivation, lose steam, lose discipline, and would become another "W" to him.

Well, not this time! I had too much riding on this. I wanted to be here for my family. I wanted to live life and not be held captive by my weight. I wanted to take long walks and not have my back and knees hurt. I wanted to be able to go to a restaurant and not pray like crazy that the hostess would give us a table and not a booth. I wanted to be able to sit in a chair without being gripped with fear that it would break, an embarrassment that I had suffered before. Yes, this time would be different. There was no choice. It had to be different!

I was at a low point, and I felt as though I was in a sling shot being stretched further and further back. With each pull backward, the tension grew more and more intense. The further removed I was from the health and life I wanted, the lower I felt.

But then I realized that objects which are pulled back in the sling the furthest also fly the furthest when released. And it was at the point where the slingshot could be stretched no more where my defining moment was realized. It was a beautiful dichotomy. The same place was in fact two different places. My lowest moment was the same one that would propel me forward.

In the midst of all this emotional chaos and devastation was opportunity. That was the beauty of it. There was a seed of great benefit squarely in the middle of this adversity. Among all of the pain and anguish, I was given a chance to regain control of my life. It was not a promise of recovered health, but rather a new possibility given to me at my lowest moment. What I did with it was entirely up to me. That seed did not only exist in my defining moments, it has existed in all defining moments. In all honesty, that seed was worth all of the adversity that came with it. It gave me hope that things could change for the better and became the foundation for my weight loss. It changed the trajectory of my life - and I was going to make sure the opportunity was not wasted.

A journey began that day that would lead me down a crazy path filled with smiles, tears, laughter, joy, disappointment, and victories and would become the very ingredients for great success. It was my path and I embraced it fully. This time would be different. That brisk fall day would be my defining moment, and my life would never be the same again.

I stood at a fork in the road. One road was well traveled. The grass had been beaten down by the number of people who had passed over it before. That road was smooth, its path was clearly marked with a sense of security. But I knew in my heart that it was not secure at all.

The other road was very different. It was overgrown. Foliage ran rampantly and had become thick and overgrown. Undoubtedly, walking down this road would require more effort and discomfort than the other. I could see a few faint footprints but nothing more down this path of the unknown. I stood there for a moment replaying the day's events once more. I exhaled, then put one foot in front of the other down the road less traveled. Just like that, I was off on a new journey down a new path. As the poet Robert Frost had promised, taking that road would make all the difference in the world.

Chapter Two

Decide To Win...And Act On It!

Three frogs are sitting on a log. One decides to jump.
How many are left? Three!
–Anonymous

Later on that evening I found myself reflecting on the events of the day. After the quality time, after the laughs and special memories created at the birthday party, after the mounds of overly sauced hot wings, after the numerous handfuls of salt laden chips and sugary sodas after the third piece of birthday cake and fourth trip to the kitchen, I sat alone in a darkened room. In the midst of all that joy, love, and laughter, I was sad. It was really a microcosm of my life. On the one hand, my life was full of great relationships and good memories. I was loved and valued. Yet, in the midst of this was a sadness that visited me often. So it was very fitting that, after all the memories and photographs I managed to avoid, I was alone with my thoughts.

I successfully played the part of a happy man on the outside, but the inside was a very different story. I continuously replayed the moments of the day in my mind and was overcome with guilt, shame, and disgust for what I had done to myself. It was during that time alone in my room that I decided to make a change, a REAL change that could only come when you've hit bottom. And that is where I was, at the bottom of a downward spiral that left me at a place where the pain to stay the same far outweighed the pain to change. It was in the still darkness of that room that I realized that enough was enough and this time things would be different. In that defining, frustrating, lowest point of my life, the point that would be the foundation of some of my highest highs, I decided to win!

Deciding to win was not enough, because decisions need to be backed up by action. I sat on the edge of the bed in the gloom as my thoughts turned to previously failed attempts at weight loss. I felt like a voyager on a ship in a vast ocean battling the onslaught of waves and rushing water. Seeds of doubt, anxiety, and fear attacked my mind as I saw that ship sink in my mind. I had not even started yet, and already I found myself in the midst of combat. I had already abandoned the ship and jumped overboard. Fear took me down and doubt was doing its best to keep me submerged beneath the water.

To me, the fight in my mind was far worse than any physical battle, as my very will was under attack. After all, this wasn't my first attempt at losing weight. While the gale force winds of chaos swirled around in my head, picked up pieces of my past, and placed them in front of my eyes, I was reminded that the past was just that- the past. No matter what happened now, it could not be altered, there was no way to go back in time and undo anything.

It was then that I realized that if the past was unchangeable and didn't matter, then why was I putting so much energy worrying about it? The failures, the bad eating, the recklessness of my bad habits did not matter. What *did* matter was how I would respond *now*. I grasped that concept and held on to it for dear life!

So I took another vital step that night. As the shackles of guilt began to fall away, I forgave myself for the past, and the drowning sailor was given a life preserver. I reached for it, slipped it on, and refused to take it off. Instead of having to struggle to keep my head above water, I was able to calmly remain afloat in that vast ocean. I was in the same dark, empty room but for the first time that night, I could see a faint light, a glimmer of hope.

If my past failures didn't matter, then the slate was clean! All that was important now was what I did next. I could now look at my past as an opportunity to find out what worked, and what didn't. But, I no longer had to stay there and be beaten down by guilt and embarrassment. I decided to win the war against obesity.

But now what? I knew decisions alone would not be enough. Without action, a moment would become a day, and the day weeks, and then months, and then what? My inaction would find me in the same predicament a year from now, maybe even worse off and further away from my goal.

This was a classic case of the old frog adage; if three frogs are sitting on a log and one decides to jump, how many frogs remain on the log? The answer, of course, is three because the frog only *decided* to jump, it didn't actually jump. I was determined to never be that frog. I would jump!

I began by taking inventory of my past attempts at losing weight to figure out what went wrong. At first, I searched for complex reasons for my failures, some combination of factors that caused my lack of success. But the more I searched, the more I realized that my setbacks resulted from nothing more than simple inaction.

With this one realization, the darkness lifted further, the blanket of despair slowly rose to reveal a light that brought with it a sense of confidence I hadn't felt in quite some time. In order to win, I had to take action and keep taking action if I was to meet my goal of a healthier me. I recognized that the only person that could stop me was me, a realization that simultaneously liberated me and filled me with anxiety. It was becoming clearer by the minute that this time around I needed to focus on the mental aspect of losing weight, because it was my mind that would drive my actions.

I never had an issue with exercising, but it was the game of mental ping pong I played in my mind that was exhausting me. I wanted chips, but I should eat fruit. More often than not, I would choose the chips, which then led to guilt and feelings of failure. Sadly, it only took a few wrong choices to derail my entire plan. But not this time. This time, I decided to win and more importantly, I now understood how.

As long as I kept taking action, success was inevitable. This resolve gave me a feeling that was very different from those I'd experienced before. I felt invincible. I was superman, defending the city of Metropolis from evil villains.

In order to maximize my new understanding, I decided right then to start piecing together a plan. What would I do? When would I work out? I began to feel overwhelmed, but reminded myself that all I had to do was take action every day; and my action for this first day was to set a goal.

Lose one hundred pounds.

There it was. I now had a clear and concise goal that I could target and focus on every day. I reveled in the moment for a while, and I had to laugh.

A few moments ago I was in the middle of a dance floor at an epic pity party. Now, here I sat, telling myself I was going to lose one hundred pounds. I don't know where the number came from. There was no magic calculation, just a feeling that the number was right, and easy, and achievable.

Still I didn't believe I could do it. But this time, there was a voice in my head that told me to never stop taking action. And that's when it clicked. The goal wasn't the important thing. Rather, it was the action to get to the goal that was vital. If I focused on the goal, then doubt and unbelief would enter into my mind. But, I knew that I could follow a plan, because the past had shown me that follow-through always yielded results and pounds were lost.

There was another click! The plan was important but what was of even more value was my mentality about losing weight. There needed to be a resolve that no matter what, I would stick with the plan. Regardless of what life threw my way, I would stay in the fight. Yes, the plan was important but my persistence, determination, and perseverance was even more important!

So in that room, as the darkness gave way to light, I made a promise to myself that I could not, would not stop. There were only two options, win the battle or quit. So I vowed I would not quit, leaving victory as my only real option. At that moment, I knew that I would succeed.

Why? Because winning was the only option I gave myself. Without realizing it, I had arrived at the threshold of a major milestone. No longer would I use diets to lose weight. Instead, I would focus on healthy living, a pivotal decision that would prove to save me from myself later on.

For the first time in a long time, I was really smiling. The tears had dried, my head was no longer down, and the pity party had come to an end. The music of despair that blared so loudly from the speakers of my mind had been silenced, the station had been changed. Replacing that music were songs of hope, renewal, and a life brimming with endless possibilities. My future was going to be amazing, the decision had been made and the goal was clear. My only option was winning.

I entered that dark room beaten down and burned by my past, but as I stood up and made my way to the door, I left a different person. Physically, I was the same, but mentally, I had turned a corner, flipped a switch. For the first time in long time there was a hint of excitement about the days that awaited me.

I was ready to face the challenges before me head on! I glanced back at the room one last time, and it's funny how, now, it didn't seem that dark at all. I smiled, closed the door, and went downstairs to rejoin my family for the remainder of the evening. I headed to the kitchen to get something to drink. With an ice-filled cup in my hand, I looked at the various sodas on the counter. As I picked up a half-full bottle of Mountain Dew, I remembered my vow. I was now a different person and I knew it.

"What you drinking?" someone asked me. "Good old water," was my response, "good old water."

Chapter 3

In The Starting Blocks

Though no one can go back and make a brand new start, anyone can start from now and make a brand new ending.
– Carl Bard

BUZZ! BUZZ! BUZZ!

The annoyingly loud and cantankerous monster of an alarm clock interrupted the peace and stillness of my bedroom, its shrill clarion call immediately pulling me from a pleasant dream world. Normally, I would negotiate for five more minutes of sleep, and five would quickly become thirty. But not today, this morning was different. There would be no pleading for five more minutes as I retreated further underneath the cover as this new day dawned.

Instead I sprang out of bed filled with excitement and anticipation of the day ahead. This was the proverbial first day of the rest of my life, and the beginning of my healthy lifestyle. Looking in the mirror, I saw the newest member of the local health club, replete with treadmills, elliptical machines, weights and many other calorie-burning devices. I was ready to use every machine at my disposal. Before I could dive head first into this new lifestyle, a starting point had to be determined.

I once heard that in order to take a trip, one needed to know two things – one's current location and the destination. Without knowing those two things, the chances of having a successful trip were slim to none. (And slim was walking out the door!) And so I had to find my starting point if I were to officially start my journey to lose one hundred pounds. The task sounded rather simple; however, it was completely opposite. Feelings of anticipation and excitement that filled me a mere few moments ago traded places with some familiar ones. Fear gripped me like never before, and anxiety nestled up to me like an old friend. The decision to lose weight was one thing, but actually finding out how much I weighed was horrifying.

After turning off the alarm, I made my way to the bathroom and while the world was still asleep, I stood on the cold floor staring at the scale. My only companion at that hour was the moon dancing behind the clouds one last time before it exchanged pleasantries with the sun and ended its shift. It shouldn't have been that much of a struggle. All I needed to do was stand on the scale and see what it said. In my mind, it really was as easy as that but, in my heart, there was far more to it than that. Years of neglect and failure bolted my feet to the floor rendering me incapable of moving.

Even more sobering was the fact that this number would really make me come face to face with myself. Whatever the scale said would force me to be honest with myself, honest about where I was and where I wanted to go. That frightened me more than I could have imagined. Being completely vulnerable was terrifying, and yet, it had to be done. I looked at the scale and tried once again to stand on the platform but my feet continued to protest. They gripped the floor with the strength that comes from adrenaline and terror. My eyes shifted from the scale to the mirror, where I saw a scared young man whose palms were cold and clammy from the ordeal.

What was the big deal, I wondered? Then it hit me. That scale would no longer allow me to break the eleventh commandment – thou shalt not lie to thy self. This would be the foundation for my weight loss and overall healthy lifestyle - and that was my issue with the scale that morning.

By stepping on the scale, I would no longer be able to lie to myself. Even in the mirror, with the truth staring at me, I was able to avoid the truth and justify what I saw. I would look with sadness and shame at my reflection and say, "Antuan, you're not that size. It's the lighting, or maybe it's the way you're standing. You know the mirror adds pounds to your frame."

Those statements were all lies; yet I repeated those untruths to myself in an effort to become numb to the emotional pain of my weight.

Yes, that was why taking this step was so hard. Confronting me was a very uncomfortable truth. But it had to be done, so with my eyes closed I stepped on the scale. For a while, I refused to open my eyes. My heart was racing and I could feel the tears pushing against the inside of my eyelids just like the waves of the ocean beating against a levee during a hurricane, certain to rush down my face once my eyes opened. Finally, with all the strength I could muster, I pried them open and forced my head downward so that I could see the damage.

-ERR-

That's what the scale said. I knew what it meant but I refused to believe it. Instead, I chose to believe the scale was broken or defective. But deep down inside I knew the truth. I stepped off and sat on the side of the bath tub with the scale manual in my hand and my fingers made their way to the troubleshooting section. My eyes slowly scanned down the page and soon locked in on those three letters – ERR.

As I began reading the manual, I understood there was no need to finish reading the explanation. Only two words were necessary to confirm what I already knew in my heart. Those two words, "weight exceeded," punched me right in the gut. But this time my reaction was not one of hopelessness but relief. I had started, and even though I still didn't know my starting weight, at least I was willing to face my fear and find out what it was, which was another milestone. I was finally being honest with myself. As I reveled in the fact that I didn't have an emotional breakdown, I remembered that there was a scale at work that I could use.

My plan was to get to work early so I could step on and off the scale before the morning wave of coworkers found their way to the cafeteria and ordered breakfast. I remembered thinking, "Who was the genius that put something so private in such a public place?" Nevertheless, I continued undaunted as I prepared for work and left the house earlier than normal. The morning radio show was replaced with a pep talk during my commute. The conversation was a full-fledged "I can do this, I better not back out, I hope and pray nobody is in the cafeteria" dialogue. The entire fifteen minute drive was one of constant mental and vocal banter.

As I entered the parking lot, the lack of cars seemed to confirm my decision. Encouraged, I opened the car door at almost the same time I put my vehicle in park. In no time, the door was closed and I was half way across the lot. My badge scanned, the door opened, and I found myself praying as I walked the hallway.

I really needed that cafeteria to be empty. I went through the double doors and looked in. Much to my chagrin, the place was full of people – not what I had hoped to see. At that point, a decision had to be made, because I knew that if I didn't step on that scale, I would simply circle the mountain one more time, and that was not what I needed. What I wanted to do was lose a hundred pounds and be able to be free from pain when I walked, to run and play with my daughter and actually enjoy the physical activity. When the things I wanted came to my mind, getting on the scale seemed less of a challenge.

So I did it. I ran in the cafeteria and placed my bags by the scale as I slid my shoes off. I closed my eyes again and stepped on the scale. In that moment, my mind painted the picture like a scene from a movie. The entire cafeteria stopped. Conversations paused and all eyes were now directed my way. In reality, no one noticed I was standing on the scale, the world did not stop spinning, and daily routines were carried on as normal. It took a few seconds, but I gathered the courage and looked down at the scale.

The three numbers before me seemed so trivial, but they meant everything to me. In that moment, I accepted where I was, squarely in the starting blocks getting ready to run my race. As I stared at the screen, an overwhelming sense of accomplishment came over me and a weight was lifted from of my shoulders. Now in my possession were the two things needed for a successful journey. I already knew where I wanted to go, but now I knew where I was starting.

I saw myself as a sprinter, focused in his lane and awaiting the sound of the starting gun. I often wondered what those moments waiting for the starter's pistol to report the beginning of the race felt like for sprinters. As they positioned themselves into the starting block, I imagined them visualizing their race one last time, and that's exactly what I did. My race was not a sprint, and my lane wasn't going to be straight, but like them, I sank into the starting block and dug in my heels.

I visualized how I would look one hundred pounds lighter and lifted my head much like a runner in the ready position. My starting block was a scale that displayed three numbers. Three numbers that would help me have a clean start.

432

At that moment, the starting gun sounded and I was off. Track and field was never my forte, but I knew that the first stride in the race was the most important. By pushing off the starting blocks with strength, the sprinter could generate enough force for quick acceleration that would carry on throughout the race. And that was what those three numbers did for me. They gave me an opportunity for a strong push off. Even more, those numbers gave me a solid base for moving forward.

As I made my way to my desk that morning, I realized that a big deal was made over a small matter. My journey had a destination, but a starting point was needed. It really was quite simple; yet determining my starting point wasn't easy. It required being honest with myself regardless of the horrific and insurmountable fear I felt. I embraced it, stepped on the scale, and my journey officially began. Finding out my starting weight was the first action that backed up my decision to lose weight, and yet another indicator that I would be successful.

As I passed through yet another door in the building, I came across another opportunity for action. I pressed the up arrow button on the elevator. As I waited I chuckled, because I had walked by the stairs to get where I now stood. The sense of pride that I felt by being honest with myself made me feel as though I could do anything. The bell sounded, the elevator doors opened and I greeted my coworkers as they made their way out of the elevator. I stood, looked where I had gone a hundred times before, and turned back, heeding the small inner voice that said, "I think I'll take the stairs!"

Chapter Four

What Do You See?

The only thing worse than being blind is having sight but no vision.
– Hellen Keller

As I sat in the empty gym parking lot, memories from days earlier sprang to the forefront of my mind. A few short weeks separated me from the anguish of finding my starting point. Now, the initial days of my journey found me preparing to work out before 5:00 AM. I hadn't lost a hundred pounds, but that didn't stop the pride from welling up inside me. At no point in those first weeks did I give in to the desire to wave the white flag and surrender; even though I questioned whether the pain of going back was worse than the pain of being disciplined and moving forward.

In my mind, I was still the same person I was when I was younger, both athletic and healthy. Yet, with each glance around at the chiseled bodies of those working out around me, I wondered if I even belonged in the gym. My self-consciousness provided far more resistance than the heaviest weight ever could.

I'd like to say the predawn workouts resulted from pure dedication to my new lifestyle, but the truth is that I thought exercising at that hour of the day would give me the best chance of avoiding the fitness buffs that seemed to overrun the gym every afternoon. Getting up for those early morning sweat sessions quickly became habit as I further distanced myself from the person I was when I started my journey. I didn't look or feel thinner, but emotionally I was as light as a feather. Those insecurities that weighed me down were being shed and replaced with self-respect and pride that gave me the fuel to keep me going.

So this particular morning, I stood taller and held my head higher as I walked towards the gym. I smiled and marveled at the progress I was making mentally, secure in the knowledge that eventually my progress would show up outside as well.

As soon as the gym doors opened, the familiar sound of the vacuum welcomed me, accompanied by a smile and a wave from the lady who was doing the vacuuming. But today, she turned off the vacuum and walked towards me.

"Hey, Antuan, it must be going on five o'clock." Without giving me an opportunity to reply, she glanced at the clock and said "Yes, it sure is! I can set my watch by you. You're doing great! How much have you lost?"

"Right around fifteen or twenty pounds," I responded. "Oh wow! That is so fantastic! You make me want to lose weight. Keep up the good work. I'm proud of you." Before I could say thank you, she flashed that warm and encouraging smile once more and returned to her duties.

There were only three people in the gym and we all said hello with a quick nod of the head. That was our way of acknowledging the sacrifices and commitment we were all making. We didn't exercise together, but there was a mutual respect for each other and what we were accomplishing.

I placed my things in a locker and headed to the door when my feet stopped abruptly and shock spread across my face as I looked at the reflection in the mirror. It had been more than a handful of years since I could stand in front of a mirror and not cringe but today I was able to take time and study the reflection. While I wasn't satisfied with what I saw, I couldn't help but be inspired by the budding changes.

There were small traces of progress in my appearance for sure, but it was an internal difference I noticed more. Sure, my face was subtly slimmer and clothes a bit looser, but it was the intangible changes that stuck out more. The sadness, despair, and quiet desperation that once filled my eyes had been replaced with joy, hope, and faith in the vision I cast for my health and well-being the night of the birthday party.

I was unable to break the gaze with the man in the mirror. He had courage, strength, and resolve. He even had a slight smile on his face! This was the same person who quietly sat in that dark room with me and whispered "You can do this. You can beat obesity. You can win." I saw how I wanted to look and feel in that room that night. I developed a mental picture of how I would look that night. Now, weeks later, he reappeared in the mirror and I was beginning to resemble the vision I had for myself.

In that moment, I was reminded of my favorite scene from the movie *The Lion King*. Simba was the son of King Mufasa but ran away because he thought he was responsible for his father's death.

When Rafiki, a friend of the royal family, tells Simba that his dad is still alive, he excitedly follows Rafiki in hopes of being reunited. Disappointment fills Simba when he realizes his dad is not alive. However, with Rafiki's guidance, Simba soon realizes that his father continues to live inside him, because Mufasa had instilled in his son the regal qualities and characteristics he himself possessed.

Rafiki: Look down there.

Simba: That's not my father. That's just my reflection.

Rafiki: No, look harder.

[He touches the water. As it ripples, Simba's reflection changes to that of his father.]

Rafiki: You see? He lives in you.

Mufasa's ghost: Simba.

Adult Simba: Father?

Mufasa's ghost: Simba, you have forgotten me.

Adult Simba: No. How could I?

Mufasa's ghost: You have forgotten who you are and so have forgotten me. Look inside yourself, *Simba.* You are more than what you have become. You must take your place in the Circle of Life.

In that scene, Simba wrestled with who he was and who he was, because he knew that we all carry a duality within us. On the one hand, he was a scared lion filled with doubt, guilt, shame, fear, and unbelief looking to escape his past mistakes and poor choices.

Yet, that very same lion was the sole heir and rightful king of Pride Rock.

How could Simba be both a king and a nomad? How could he be a fierce warrior and run at the first sign of trouble? Was he the reflection in the water or the lion looking in the water? I posed that same question to myself countless times.

Was I the guy I in the locker room mirror or was I the guy looking in the mirror? Was I someone paralyzed with failure or a person who possessed a steely resolve? The answer to those questions was both. Just as Simba was both lions I was both people. That scene taught me a valuable lesson - the difference between facts and truth.

The facts were, Simba had abandoned his family, played a role in his father's death, and was living a life unfitting of the King of Pride Rock. His life was rife with pain, agony, and anguish. Those were the facts.

The truth, however, was different. He was the true king of Pride Rock and had all the rights, power, privilege, and authority that come with such a title. He was strong, fearless, courageous, and full of valor.

I was the fact-filled Simba as I dealt with the same things he did. My bad decisions and failed weight loss attempts caused me to run far away. I looked harder in the mirror and my truth became crystal clear. I was powerful beyond measure, fully capable of winning this fight, and once I completely understood that truth, I was ready to return to my weight loss journey just as Simba returned to Pride Rock to take control of his kingdom. Only in my case, the sovereign realm I needed to return to was my health, and I regained control with the confidence of knowing what I was and who I was in spite of what the facts seemed to be.

To be honest, there were times when the facts appeared much more real than the truth. There were days when I was overwhelmed by them. It was on those days that I focused on the vision I had for my health.

Without that vision, I would have quit. But it was that very sight which was vital to my success. It allowed me to focus on my truth even when the facts were screaming at me to ignore it. I had to meditate on what the results looked like. I had to meditate on what the results felt like. The more I "looked harder," the more I realized that I possessed everything I needed to win. There were seeds of greatness inside me the entire time. I simply needed to discover them. And they were attached to my truth, and my truth was tied to the vision I had.

As a result of that realization, I discovered more about me with each obstacle I faced and realized why the guy in the mirror was smiling. He knew he had already won the battle because seeds of perseverance, resilience, and discipline were being cultivated in him each day. If victory escaped me momentarily and defeat seemed to have me firmly in its grasp, I knew I would keep going because I hadn't reached my destination.

Whenever I felt the facts dominating my thoughts, I remembered Rafiki and Simba at the river on that clear, dark night in the jungle. If my truth was clouded from my sight, I knew it was okay. I simply looked again. I looked harder and the reflection of truth about me became clearer.

It was only a few days later that this new resolve would be tested. On that day, I saw the guy in the mirror. I was on the treadmill, early in my workout, when the thoughts of quitting came to me again. I was already sleepy, drained, and didn't want to be in the gym. No doubt the rigors of the day had gotten to me. I pushed on for a few more minutes until the idea of quitting early, and cheating myself in the process, seemed inevitable.

Then I glanced up and noticed a mirror in front of the treadmill. Immediately I met his gaze. Amazingly, the look in his eyes was the complete opposite of how I felt. I was tired, lacking focus, and ready to quit. Yet the look in his eyes was one of determination, encouragement, and perseverance. He even had that same smile on his face! My lungs were on fire, but the man in the mirror was running on the treadmill and smiling as if to say "That's right, you see it! You're running! Don't you quit!"

Before I knew it six minutes had become fifteen, then twenty, then twenty-five. Thoughts of quitting were replaced with thoughts of how far I had come. The guy in the mirror had a look of steely resolve and pride in what he was doing. So much so I increased the speed and incline to levels I had never attempted. I was uncertain if I could do it but I did know that if I kept looking in *those* eyes, I would be able reach new heights.

And I did! I pushed myself for the last ten minutes. I was out of breath, and my lungs felt like they would burst. Sweat poured out of my body profusely, and the only thing I could think was, "I did it!" Another milestone had been accomplished.

I wiped my face and threw the towel in the hamper and I looked back in the mirror to see the man look back at me with a smile, nodding in approval and saying, "I told you it could be done." I glanced in his eyes once more and said, "I'll see you tomorrow." I looked harder in the mirror and replied, "Absolutely you will!"

Chapter Five

Victory Loves Preparation

It's not the will to win that matters - everyone has that.
It's the will to prepare to win that matters.
-Paul "Bear" Bryant

Two pounds gained!

Long after the scale's display went blank, the number continued to flash before my eyes like the bright red neon lights on Broadway. The scale had to be wrong. I had been losing weight consistently, and this week should have been no different. I had seen this movie every week and knew exactly how it ended; nine pounds lost, four pounds lost, six pounds lost. Each time I watched it, it concluded with me losing weight- nine pounds, then four pounds. How could this week's movie end any differently?

I had developed a great routine that culminated with Saturday weigh-ins. I would exercise four to five days during the week then reap the rewards of my sacrifice and discipline on Saturday mornings. My routine was foolproof and meticulous, or so I thought. To say I was a creature of habit was an understatement. Every week I weighed in on the same day at the same time wearing the same clothes.

Armed with the knowledge of how wonderful my plan was, there was no doubt I would lose weight this week as well. It wasn't a matter of *if* but *how much* would be lost.

I was still in shock as I stepped off the scale and began recalibrating it. That was the only logical explanation for my weight gain. Still in denial, I weighed once more expecting to see a different result, the *real* one this time. But once again, the result was the same, both real and unwanted.

In times past, a day like that Saturday would have led down a slippery slope ending with my surrender. However this morning, instead of falling off the wagon, I let the shock subside and took a step back, collected my thoughts, and thought about what had allowed me to experience my initial success. I needed to know why I gained weight this week.

In the early days of my journey, I did everything I was supposed to do. My workouts were consistent and my food choices were healthier. So I searched through my food and exercise logs in hopes of finding clues as to what went wrong. And there it was – I had only worked out twice. Without realizing it, I had become a victim of my own success and allowed complacency to creep into my routine.

But not only did my false sense of security affect my workouts, it had found its way into my food choices as well. As I looked at my entries for the week and I saw more reasons for my weight gain. Snacks full of fresh vegetables and fruit had been replaced with potato chips and artificially fruit flavored candy. Iced tea and soda showed up in my logs far more than water. Yes, complacency had left its fingerprints all over my discipline and decisions that week.

Success always left clues, and my log entries shone a bright light on them. But it wasn't enough to stop there. I needed to figure out why I made those poor choices to be sure I would make the right choices going forward. My desire to lose weight hadn't waned nor had my motivation to do so decreased. So what was it? Was it too much confidence? Was I reveling too much in the moment and not keeping my eye on the bigger picture? I answered those questions with a lot of self-honesty and vulnerability.

Yes. That was the answer.

I wasn't as disciplined as I needed to be and somehow had allowed myself to focus on the few pounds I had lost instead of concentrating on the goal I set. The answer to those questions was merely a canary in a coal mine – an early warning sign of trouble to come if I continued down this path; a path that lacked proper preparation.

That was it! That was the real reason for those two pounds. Failure found me that week because I wasn't proactive and staying on the offensive. I reflected on the previous week's events and realized that I had neglected to fix my lunch one day hadn't laid out my workout clothes for an early morning session on another. Those missed opportunities reduced my chances of success and, as a result, I gained two pounds.

A lesson was learned that day – having a desire to win was not enough. I had to have a desire to *prepare* to win. More importantly, if I didn't prepare, I was automatically planning to fail. When I started my journey, I brought my lunch to work and packed my workout clothes so they were easily available. The same could not be said about my week of failure. If I were going to get back on track, I would have to go back to those habits of the first few weeks. I did not want another week like this, so I placed an emphasis on preparing myself for the next day every night.

Instead of watching television or surfing the internet during my down time, I began fixing my lunch and snacks. I'd make sure my workout clothes were placed neatly on the chair in my bedroom so I wouldn't have to search for them when the alarm clock sounded. Those small steps created a wave of momentum that I rode all the way to the next weigh in.

The following Saturday I found myself in the same clothes at the same time standing on the same scale. This time, the movie ended much better. The scale showed a five pound loss and once again all was well in my world. I nodded in approval but didn't stay in that place too long. There was no benefit to smiling or patting myself on the back. Instead, I headed downstairs to the kitchen and started making a shopping list of the food I needed for the upcoming week.

Those two pounds taught me a valuable lesson, and one I revisit often. If you fail to prepare, you're inevitably preparing to fail.

Chapter Six

Position Yourself To Win

The greatest way to face tomorrow's problems is to prepare for it today.
- John Maxwell

Aromas of spices and steam infused with savory scents of roasted chicken topped with a creamy sauce competed for my attention while I patiently waited for the lunch line to progress. The protective glass that covered the buffet was ill equipped to thwart the advance of the fragrances that traveled from the warming trays to my nose. Each one lingered in the air, dancing back and forth, beckoning me to throw in the towel and dine with them.

A smile quickly spread across my face. I thought to myself, "Nope. You won't get me today! I'm so much stronger than this. I'm losing weight consistently. No derailing my quest."

I was completely focused on my goals and there was no way I would give in that day. Realizing the futility of their efforts, the delightful aromas retreated and the line moved forward. With confidence in my mind and card in hand, the cashier gave me my total.

"$2.84, Antuan" she said. I began to slide my card and stopped mid-swipe. "You know what? Add a cookie please. Those chocolate chip cookies are amazing!" She quickly agreed, "Yes! And these are fresh out of the oven so they're still warm. Mmmm. So good!" And just like that; with salad, water, and a cookie on my tray, another lesson began.

I sat at the table and began to eat my lunch. While biting into the cookie, guilt and shamed filled my head. The pride from navigating the buffet minutes earlier was now gone. The confidence I wore like a coat was nowhere to be found. How in the world did this cookie get here? I did all the right things. I didn't give into earlier temptations and resisted the calorie-laden enticements of the various entrees. Yet, there I sat with a half-eaten chocolate chip cookie in my hand and the sting of defeat in my heart.

"How in the world did I get here?" That question echoed in my mind as I finished my lunch. As I thought about it, the answer became clear. I gave great attention to prepping meals and exercising but I completely ignored planning for the critical moments – those hidden snares that lay dormant as I innocently enter the trap. They are subtle and never announce their arrival. They appear harmless at first glance but are fatal if you walk into them.

While a cookie here or a missed workout there may not derail my journey, I realized that, compounded over time, those decisions will slowly close around me and completely ensnare me, rendering escape from the many traps laid for me impossible.

I unwound from the day's events that evening and my thoughts were still on that cookie. While sitting in my favorite chair twirling a quarter between my fingers, I realized my preparation was just like that coin. Just as the quarter has two sides, so does my planning. The head of the planning coin deals with the best case scenarios while the tail side focuses on the trap I had experienced earlier. If either side is not properly addressed, then I won't be equipped for success.

In order to ensure I was ready for any situation that could arise, I had to identify and create a strategy for the snares before me. What scenarios would pull me away from my dreams and goals? After a quick analysis, I figured out that my pitfalls came from two things; going to bed late and not preparing my meals for the next day. The cookie incident resulted from my failure to bring lunch to work that day. Skipped morning workouts happened because after five or six hours of sleep, hitting the snooze button was much easier than getting up.

How would I deal with those situations in the future? The answer to that question would have far more impact on my success than I ever realized. I had to determine my response before I found myself in those circumstances again.

It was impossible for me to avoid all the traps because life happens and hectic schedules can force quick and unexpected decisions. There was no guarantee I would get eight hours of sleep nightly. Nor could I ensure I would always make my meals prior to going to work.

Instead of focusing on avoiding the many pitfalls that awaited me, I decided to position myself in such a way that I would make right decisions. However, making those choices would require more discipline and commitment. So, on days I needed to eat in the cafeteria, my debit card would remain at home, replaced by exactly

$2.84 in cash. By having the correct change, I would ensure I could avoid the temptations in the lunch line.

I would place my cell phone in my tennis shoes and set them on the bathroom floor with my gym clothes on top of them so that, regardless of how tired I was, it would be too difficult for me to snooze. After going through the trouble of waking up, digging out the phone, and silencing the alarm, going back to bed would be useless. By the time I reached the phone, I would be at the point of no return and would go to the gym regardless of how many hours I had slept.

The convenience of making bad decisions was eradicated as much as possible, leaving me with only the right decision to make. At first, it seemed strange to put forth so much effort into situations that rarely occurred. Most days, I didn't find myself in those dangerous circumstances. But big doors swing on small hinges and if I hoped to lose a hundred pounds, I had to be committed to making the right decisions in those small, seemingly trivial decisions during those rare moments.

Committing to those small things was simple but not easy. Yet the rewards were worth it. By making it difficult to make the wrong choice, I was better positioned to win and gave myself a chance to keep succeeding. As long as I had a chance, I would keep fighting.

I learned how to get out of my own way; a way that would add a chocolate chip cookie to my lunch nine out of ten times, the same way that would help me retreat to the comfort of my bed for a few more minutes of sleep instead of going to the gym for an early morning workout. Preparing for both sides of the coin made a huge difference.

Weeks later I found myself sitting in the same chair at the same table in the cafeteria. This time the cookie had been replaced with an apple. A coworker sat down next to me and the conversation drifted to my noticeable weight loss. "What have you been doing?" he asked. I responded with the standard reply I would give when I didn't know if the person really wanted to know the answer.

My response was "I've been eating better and exercising." "I need to do something. I need to get a handle on my health." he said.

"You can do it. If I can, I know you can." For just a moment, I saw a fleeting glimmer of hope in his eyes. As quickly as it appeared, I could see the doubt and negative self-talk cause it to vanish.

"I don't know, Antuan. I try to eat healthy but it's so hard. I bring my lunch but end up not wanting it as soon as I smell the food in the cafeteria." I was ready to respond but before I had a chance, he got up from the table and said he would be right back.

He returned with a cookie in his hand. "These things right here," he said as he waved it around, "Will be what holds me back. These things are phenomenal!" I looked at him and smiled. "Friend, the cookie isn't the problem."

He looked at me with an expression of bewilderment on his face. I took out a penny that was in my pocket and smiled as I held it in my hand. As I placed the penny down on the table in front of him, I asked "Do you mind if I tell you about both sides of this coin?"

Chapter Seven

Recognizing Success

Success is a journey, not a destination. The doing is often more important than the outcome.
-Arthur Ashe

The workouts were challenging this particular week. Spurred by consecutive weeks of less than desired weight loss, the decision was made to increase the intensity of my exercise regimen. I focused with laser-like precision on my meals. Every serving of protein, carbohydrates, and vegetables was carefully planned and measured. The cheat meals were nonexistent during the next seven days. This would be the week that I lost more than one pound!

It was inconceivable to me that I would not lose at least five or six pounds this week. I woke up early this Saturday morning eager to weigh in so I could relish my certain breakthrough. With each step closer to the scale, the anticipation grew as I could feel the fat melting away. I stood on the scale and surveyed the bathroom while allowing the scale to tell me what I already knew. How many pounds would I lose this week? Four pounds lost would be fine. Six pounds would be better. The longer I stayed on the scale, the more I figured nine pounds lost would be the perfect outcome.

"Wait, why not ten?" I asked myself. Surely the spoils of victory would be ten pounds. I returned from my daydream long enough to look down at the scale, and couldn't believe my eyes. There was no way the scale was right!

I had lost less than a pound in seven days. I stepped down from the scale and let it reset itself. I thought, "The scale probably needs to be calibrated again. I remember moving it two millimeters to the left before I got on it, so that must be it."

Once again, I returned to the scale and saw the same result – only three fourths of a pound lost. I stood there in disbelief, like a boxer who had just lost a fixed fight.. This bout had to be rigged because, in my mind, that was the only reasonable answer.

I knew I had out-boxed my opponent. I also knew I had gotten more points, and done it in style. There were no cuts on my face and he hadn't hurt me at any time during the fight. Never was my back against the ropes.

I shook my head and muttered under my breath. "The judges got this one wrong, man. Unbelievable." That number was well below my expectations. To add insult to injury, the meticulously measured meals and exhausting workouts did not result in even a single pound of weight loss!

Amazingly, there was no long period of sulking this time around. While I wanted better results, a loss was still a loss no matter how small. I shrugged it off and went about my day.

A few hours later I was with my family waiting to be seated at a local restaurant. Laughter and pleasant conversation filled our little corner of the lobby as we waited for a table. When the pager finally vibrated alerting us that it was time, we made our way to the hostess station and a bubbly young lady greeted us with a warm smile.

"Right this way guys. Your booth is ready." Wait, a booth? Did I hear her correctly? Fear and dread filled my body as my heart crashed into the bottom of my stomach with a force that only enraged the butterflies already there.

Immediately my mind went back to an unpleasant time and place, for it was only a few short years ago that we sat in a booth. On that night, there was no room between my protruding stomach and the edge of the table. The pressure of being squeezed as I sat in that booth produced beads of sweat that slid down my face as if it were a waterslide. The restaurant was not hot at all, yet I exerted so much energy trying to force myself into the limited space that a small puddle of sweat formed on the table.

I was so embarrassed that I was unable to return my wife's concerning glances. She looked at me and knew how uncomfortable and embarrassed I was. At that moment, I just wanted to crawl in a hole and never come out. That moment scarred me and was forever etched in mind. Years would pass, multiple visits to restaurants would come and go but the memory of that booth remained. Each time we ate at a restaurant, I made sure that we sat at a table.

And so these were the thoughts that occupied my mind as our hostess led us to our booth. With each step, my heart beat faster and my legs grew heavier. I had not sat in a booth since that fateful day several years ago and I was terrified.

"Here you are. Your waitress will be with you shortly." My wife and daughter sat down rather quickly and started perusing the menu. I, on the other hand, remained standing. I was not at all prepared for what awaited. I stared at that empty space. Unsure of what to do next, I started to sit down. As soon as I began to sit, I stopped.

"What am I going to do?" I thought. I had seen this movie before and knew how it ended. There was no alternate ending. Its conclusion was sweat, embarrassment, and a concerned look from my wife.

Unfortunately, I knew I would have to sit down at some point, but I was scared to do so. However, if our fun evening was to continue I would have to take my seat in that small unforgiving booth. I would have to wedge myself into that confined space at some point.

My knees slowly bent as my feet led me to the table. With closed eyes and a slight tremble in my legs, I took a deep breath and cautiously made my way to the booth. My hands ran along the edge of the table and guided me in. I did not want to open my eyes – and why should I open them? There was no need because that look of concern on my wife's face was permanently engrained in my mind. Were it possible, my eyes would have remained closed throughout dinner. But that was not an option, so without hurry I opened my eyes.

When I did, shock, disbelief, and astonishment greeted me. My brain analyzed what my eyes saw. Confused, they darted from right to left, left to right, up and down, and down and up.

What did I see? Space! Empty space existed between me and the table. The room between my stomach and the table belied what the scale had spoken only hours earlier. I was speechless.

I motioned to my wife. At first, she didn't understand. I managed to utter one word – a simple one syllable word.

"Look," I said as I gestured with my eyes and hands to the inches that gaped between me and the table. A broad smile swiftly spread across her face. Her eyes were joyous as she realized what had happened. Right there, in that restaurant, I understood that success was not solely based on the scale.

When I started down this path of losing weight and becoming healthier, my success was completely based on the numbers displayed on the scale. That viewpoint did not always work in my favor. Although the scale was a good way to measure results, it was a very fickle and misleading creature. Very rarely did the scale give a complete picture of my progress. Each time the scale fluctuated between marginal weight loss and marginal weight gain, my emotions and thoughts hung on for the ride. That rollercoaster provided me with enough angst and emotional instability to consider quitting multiple times. More importantly, it blinded me from seeing other victories.

Because I relied so heavily on the scale to measure success, I missed out on celebrating other indicators of accomplishment. The looser fitting clothes, the ability to run longer distances and lift heavier weights were all moments of triumph that I often overlooked. The scale did not capture the fact that I was now walking up and down flights of stairs without having to stop to catch my breath. The scale also failed to capture the fact that I was able to walk around the mall without my back or knees hurting. All of those things were victories worthy of celebration. By no means were these small feats. Each one required levels of discipline, effort, and sacrifice that pushed me mentally as well as physically.

Yet, they were cast aside and discarded as if they didn't matter and held no value.

But they did. Even though I failed to see it because I was looking for success in the wrong place, they were all every bit as important as that number on the scale. Later that night I wrote down all of my accomplishments that were unrelated to my weight. When I finished, I was amazed at how many things were on that sheet of paper.

Clothes sizes were dropped. Body aches were less frequent. My quality of life had increased. I was able to actually enjoy walks with my wife. We attempted to play tennis as a family. The list was endless. All of those things happened even as the scale seemed to reflect little or no progress.

The victories away from the scale weren't celebrated because I put more value on the destination than the journey. I was healthier and lighter than I had been in years, yet my mind paid more attention to a one pound loss. I realized that my personal momentum was directly affected by the scale and as a result my vision was impaired. My sight was fine but how I saw myself during those moments was cloudy. The scale told me I was not having success because of a number. But the truth was that my many achievements along the way painted a truer picture of who I was than any number on a scale could.

Who was I? I was someone who had become determined to win, transformed into a person who would not tolerate excuses from himself regardless of the challenge. The scale failed to measure intangibles such as heart, will, or effort, so I stopped giving so much credence to the scale.

I will never forget that Saturday night. I have carried the pride, tears of joy, and beaming smiles from my wife and daughter with me from that night forward. As a matter of a fact, the memory of the night began to replace the one that had dominated my thoughts from years earlier. Not only was the fear of sitting in a both gone, I actually started to look forward to sitting in a booth again. When progress stalled on the scale, I pulled out my list of milestones, went back to that night, that moment, and remembered who I had become along the way.

Why did I do that? The answer is easy. The memory of that night and my list of accomplishments truly measured my success. They showed how much despair, hopelessness, and desperation I lost – and that could never be measured by any scale.

Chapter Eight

Winds of Adversity

Adversity is like a strong wind. It tears away from us all but the things that cannot be torn, so that we see ourselves as we really are.
– Arthur Golden

One thing that assisted me in losing weight was the ability to recognize teachable moments that lay hidden beneath the surface of even the most difficult situations. These moments entered my life without much fanfare, but had I not learned how to actively seek out the lessons in the midst of adversity, I was certain to continue to experience the ups and downs with my health and wellness that I always had.

In order to maximize the impact of those lessons, I constantly asked myself the same questions. "What can I learn from this? Why am I in this situation?"

I quickly realized that I needed to actively study these difficult situations. I also came to understand that my learning shouldn't be limited to just my own circumstances. I found I could glean just as much from how others successfully handled their difficulties, as well. Some of the most profound and impactful lessons I learned came from the most unexpected places and people.

That was certainly the case with a certain ten-year-old gymnast. In just her second state meet, she placed third in her division, an impressive feat. But the road she traveled to get to that podium made the accomplishment even more inspiring.

After her first state competition, our daughter Ty sat through the medal ceremony and never heard her name called. There was no opportunity to have a medal placed around her neck and her hands raised in victory. She looked up through tear-stained eyes and listened to her coach console her before we left the meet.

"Ty, these girls were older and you held your own. You're going to work hard all summer and next year you're going to come back and kill it at state. Why? Because you're a beast!"

Over the next twelve months, I had a front row seat to the battles this little girl fought as she chased her dreams. Determined to be a champion, she constantly met disappointment and frustration with a relentless attitude. With every practice, she faced her fears by working on various skills. Ty would fall countless times from the balance beam. Sometimes she immediately sprang to her feet and other times she stayed on the mat looking at the ceiling. As she slowly made her way back onto the beam, I imagined her contemplating whether it was really worth all the bumps and bruises. Three hours later Ty would get in the car and just look out the window in silence fighting back tears. Finally she'd exhale deeply, hit her fist against the door, and break the stillness with the question, "Daddy, why can't I get this? I'm trying really hard. Maybe I'll never get it."

"Ty, you can get it. You just have to keep fighting," I'd respond as I did my best to believe for both of us. The next day she would return to practice and face her obstacles head-on. She attempted backflip after backflip after backflip until the falls became less frequent and she landed them consistently.

Ty would arrive at meets full of confidence only to have her resolve tested as she fell from the balance beam. She had to control her emotions, pull herself together and finish her routine. After all, her coaches, teammates, and judges expected her to finish regardless of the fact that she had fallen. With misty eyes and quivering lips, she'd return to the beam, flash a smile at the judges, and keep going.

I'd ask her the same question after the disappointing meets. "Do you want to quit?" Whether her face was buried in her hands or she was staring through the car window, Ty would respond with a firm "No."

I'm not sure when it happened but somewhere along the way Ty began to embrace the adversity. Her questions of doubt transformed into statements of how close she was to completing a new skill. The falls, bumps, and bruises became battle wounds she was proud to show off. She realized that difficult times were a necessary part of the process if she were going to be a champion.

All those memories flooded my mind as I saw her standing on the podium with her arms raised in victory and triumph. The smile and joy that had eluded her months earlier were present for the entire world to see. Her mother and I were filled with unbelievable pride – not because she placed so highly but rather because she fought so hard to get there.

I learned so much from Ty and her struggles. I wasn't going to be a champion gymnast but I was striving to be the best Antuan Russ. There were days when I felt things were extremely hard and wondered if it was worth it; perhaps I was destined to a life of obesity and the shackles that accompanied it. But then an image of a young gymnast falling down and getting up would appear in my mind and I knew I would win if I did the same and simply refused to lose.

Adversity is like a summer thunderstorm. The blue skies suddenly turn grey and clouds full of rain burst, unleashing torrential downpours. Then, as quickly as the rain starts, it stops, the ominous clouds dissipate and blue skies return. Hardships aren't designed to be permanent nor are they there to stifle you. Instead, they were meant to be like rain, providing what you need to grow.

In my journey, the irony was that the same stormy conditions that seemed to bring resistance and pain, also brought increased strength, resolve, and left me further along the road to a healthier me. When the winds of adversity howled and knocked me down, I rested for a moment, gathered my composure and returned to my feet.

Chapter Nine

What You Say Is What You Get

*Death and life are in the power of the tongue: and they
that love it shall eat the fruit thereof.
–Proverbs 18:21 KJV*

"I quit!"

Those were the words that echoed in my head as beads of sweat raced down my forehead and crashed into my eyes. Each gasp for breath was cut short by an increasing burning sensation in my lungs as I attempted to move my leaden legs. My eyes were nearly closed as I squinted to combat the stinging I felt while trying to catch a glimpse of the blurry red numbers on the treadmill.

Three minutes felt like thirty as I decreased my pace to a snail's crawl. I did all I could to keep going but I was losing this round. I was in the middle of a battle but it wasn't a physical one. The fight I was in had everything to do with my mind and nothing to do with the treadmill.

Internally, a debate was going on between the person I had been and the person I was becoming. Both sides stated their cases well. I listened to the voice on my left as the old me emphatically argued for the idea of hitting the red button with those four letters on it that would end my pain. He begged me to put a swift end to all the suffering.

"Antuan, stop. This is crazy! It's not worth all this. Regroup and try again another day. This just isn't your day." But before I could even consider his argument, the person I was becoming immediately told me that "another day" was not an actual day of the week.

"Nowhere on a calendar will you find another day, Antuan." I was reminded that another day turns into someday – a day where nothing is ever accomplished. He implored me to endure and remember the satisfaction of pushing past my discomfort to a place of growth.

"This is just resistance. That's how you get stronger. You meet resistance and overcome it!" "Antuan," the new me continued, "being strong has nothing to do with how much you can lift or how many muscles you have. Strength is determined by how much resistance you're able to withstand. Whether you quit or push through and finish, the pain will subside as soon as you stop. What will remain will be how you feel about what you decided to do. Will you be proud you finished or sorry you quit?"

I knew the feeling I had from finishing a run always lasted longer than the run itself. Be it pride or guilt, the emotion stayed with me. So what did I do?

I listened to the person I was becoming. What happened next was nothing short of a miracle. I finished the thirty-five minute run! It wasn't the prettiest run nor did I cover the most distance, but that didn't matter to me. All that mattered was that I finished what I started.

How did I manage to finish? I talked myself through it. Each time I look back on that morning, I laugh because I've always said that talking to yourself doesn't make crazy – answering yourself does. Well that morning, on the treadmill, not only did I talk to myself, I also answered.

Quietly I whispered, "I can do it. Just run fifteen more seconds." When those fifteen seconds passed, I told myself I could run ten more seconds. Literally, I was talking aloud and cheering. I lowered the volume on my headphones so the only thing I heard was my positive statements. Pretty soon the statements turned to questions.

"Who can do all things through Christ who strengthens him?" I would ask. "Me," was my response. Initially, my answers lacked belief but as I continued to talk to myself, they became stronger. "You got this! If you can run for thirty seconds, you can run for another fifteen."

I continued, "I can! And I will!" As my words continued to push me, my endurance increased. The run didn't become easier, I grew stronger. It has been my belief that words are tools that have the power to build or destroy. Not only are they tools, but words are also connected to both emotions and actions. That day on the treadmill was a great example of that principle.

I realized words were seeds that bore fruit – be it good or bad. When I experienced difficult times, I often spoke negatively, and those thoughts rooted themselves deeply in my psyche. Without realizing it, I was sabotaging my own efforts.

This time around I made deliberate efforts to use the power of words in my favor instead of against me. When I didn't see the numbers I wanted on the scale, I refused to give in to negative words and thoughts. Instead, words of victory, triumph, and tenacity were spoken. I always heard that what you see is what you get. I learned throughout this process that what you *say* is what you get. Learning to speak positively was one of the hardest things I did, but it made a huge difference.

After finishing that run, I made my way to the locker room where I was approached by a gentleman who had been next to me on the treadmill. He thanked me for my encouragement. I told him he was welcome but that I didn't know what he meant.

He told me, "I left my ear buds at home and have never run without music. I can't run without music. The time passes too slowly. But I needed to get my run in. Each time I decided to quit, I heard you tell me I could do it. And I could do all things through Christ."

I told him that I had no idea he was listening to me but it was an amazing feeling to know that I played a small role in his success. We laughed and he said, "Well, brother, I'm glad you were talking to yourself. It helped me out more than you'll ever know. I don't think I would've finished had you not been there."

As we walked through the locker rooms doors, I wondered what would've happened had I spoken words of defeat. I believe we both would have quit. I was glad I chose to speak positivity that morning, as it would have been just as easy to speak negative words.

That day I vowed to become just as diligent about the words I spoke to myself as I was with my nutrition and workouts. On days when discouragement was in abundance and my belief waned, I reflected on that morning in the gym and simply changed my words. I would soon find out that, after my words became positive, discouragement would leave and only belief would remain.

Chapter Ten

Three Letters...One Question

The why is more important than the how or what
- Anonymous

The sound of the high-pitched shriek once again pierced the stillness of my bedroom. As the sound grew louder and brought an end to the peace and tranquility of my sleep, my feet shuffled along in the darkness to silence it. Still in somewhat of a daze, I fought back the lethargic feelings that follow interrupted sleep and prepared for my morning workout.

The moment I opened the front door, the frigid morning temperature greeted me and promptly chased the lingering sleepiness away from me. The coldness of the night slapped me in the face repeatedly while getting in the car. Once again the moon was my traveling partner as I drove to the gym. While the rest of the world was still sound asleep, my car came to a stop in the parking lot.

I sat there and gazed through the sunroof at the moon with its soft and inviting glow. My body was at the gym but my mind and will were closer to the moon's surface than the door beyond my windshield. I was tired, and the fatigue had nothing to do with it being five o'clock in the morning. Nor did it have anything to do with only having had six hours of sleep that night. No, this was the weariness of getting up day in and day out to come to the gym. This was tired of being sore six days every week. This exhaustion was completely mental.

My hand rested on the car door for a minute or two, or three, and I had no intentions of opening it. I was perfectly content to recline my seat and go back to sleep right there in that empty parking lot. Reluctantly however, I exited the car, and made my way through the gym doors.

I knew the routine like the back of my hand – walk in the gym, scan my card, and greet the congenial woman pushing the vacuum cleaner back and forth across the worn-down brown carpet. After that, climb the stairs to the cardio equipment and walk past the row of elliptical machines, only to stop once I reached the treadmills.

I used the same treadmill for each workout. As I set it up for the cardio portion of my workout, I wondered what I was doing there. After all, there was only one other person in the gym. I thought to myself, "You can do this later. You've done well so far. You deserve a break." I pushed those thoughts out of my mind and began walking.

Starting has always been the hardest part of a workout for me, and this one was no different. Thoughts of stopping usually left after a few short minutes, but this morning they refused to leave. Not even the motivating songs blasting from my ear buds could push me to continue. The desire to quit refused to be ignored and I raised the white flag – pressing the red button in the middle of my workout. Once the treadmill came to a complete stop, I headed downstairs and made a beeline for the exit.

"Finished already? You must have gotten here super early today!" The question came from another gentleman who had come in a few minutes earlier. He was one of a handful of faithful gym patrons who also had a similar morning routine. Over the course of a few months, we grew to have a mutual respect for each other.

"I'm not leaving, just headed to the sauna," I replied. There was no way in the world I could let him see me walk out without completing my workout.

The heat from the sauna hit me like a ton of bricks as I sat down on the bench and caught my breath. Once again I found myself in a room alone with my thoughts. Unlike those times when I had just begun my journey, I was no longer miserable. My mental, physical, and emotional health were much better now due to my many victories and achievements.

So what was the issue today? How did I find myself here? I was not burnt out. Rest days were regularly scheduled into my routine. Yet, I simply didn't feel like being in the gym that morning. Normally I could distance myself from my feelings but today they blatantly disobeyed my orders to leave.

To be completely transparent, I did not feel like continuing. After all, I had lost weight, and wasn't that the goal?
Sure, it wasn't the hundred pounds I decided to lose but I had lost a significant amount of weight. I was over the entire healthy lifestyle. I didn't want to continue counting calories. I was ready to eat

anything but chicken breasts and sweet potatoes; and if I never saw another egg white, I wouldn't be sad.

Using a few towels, I created a pillow, and stretched out on the wooden bench. I asked myself the most important question that I could possibly ask myself. Up until this point, it hadn't even crossed my mind, but lying there in that sauna with closed eyes, I found the fuel that would keep me going.

Why?

The question seemed simple at first glance. However, it was anything *but* a simple question. Previously, I paid lots of attention to what needed to be done and how to do it. But never had I thought about *why* I was doing it. Interestingly enough, there were a plethora of good answers to the question, but only a few were the right ones.

So how did I pick the right answers from the merely good ones? I looked at my actions. If the answers didn't pull me along when I wanted to stop, then it was just another good answer and not the right one.

The right answer would make me cry at the thought of not completing the task. The right answer would create such an emotional pull within me that I would not be able to abandon the journey before it was done. The right answer would replace fatigue, allowing determination to remain long after the motivation faded. The right answer would ensure that I listened to the voice of discipline and not my feelings. That morning I found my "why."

My why was my family. Sure I wanted to look and feel better and yes, I wanted to have a better quality of life. Yes, I wanted to shop in the regular section of clothing stores. Those were all good answers, but they didn't keep me going. After all, I had quit all my previous attempts and had learned to live with my poor health. I learned how to deal with the pain in my back and knees, to hide shirts I was no longer able to button by wearing sweaters over them.

Feeling better, quality of life, and a better shopping experience were good, but they failed to connect with me emotionally, and that connection was vital because it sustained my drive and passion when everything in me wanted to quit. I wanted to get healthy to lower the risk of a premature death. I wanted to do all I could to ensure I did not leave behind a wife, daughter, mother, father, brother, or friends. I wanted a life full of laughter, memories of graduations, baby dedications, and retirement parties. Those things pushed and pulled me down the path towards a brand new Antuan.

In the sauna, I realized why it was so hard to get going earlier. I was on empty. I was out of fuel. Without the fuel, it was impossible to keep going. Just like a car that had run out of gas, I sputtered and eventually rolled to a complete stop. Once I stopped, I was able to get to the shoulder of the road and out of harm's way. For me, the shoulder of the road was the sauna. From the time I got up that morning, I was sputtering. By the time I hit that red button on the treadmill I was completely out of gas.

Thankfully I was able to safely make it to the shoulder of the road with a little push from my friend in the gym. Hitting that stop that morning was the best thing I could have done, because it helped me find my why. And it was the why that filled my tank.

I learned a very valuable lesson that day. It was vital to visit my why every now and then. By doing that, I kept my eyes on the bigger picture. The right answer to the why question allowed me to persevere. During hard moments and times of disappointment, I remembered the feeling I had when thinking of my family's life without me. When I wanted to skip a workout, or just go through the motions, I imagined the looks on my family's faces in the waiting room of a hospital. I saw their reaction when the doctor said, "I'm sorry, we did everything we could do but….."

Every time without fail, that refocused and realigned me with the decision I made months ago to get healthy. I opened my eyes and wiped away the sweat. Amazingly, the tiredness was replaced with a feeling of triumph. As I sat up, and I said to myself, "let's go knock this one out."

I wiped my face once more before throwing the towel in the laundry basket, and headed towards the treadmill. Once it was set up, I started jogging. To the side of me was the gentlemen with whom I had become friends. "Antuan, I knew you weren't done. Your shirt wasn't soaked." I nodded and smiled. "No, sir. I'm not finished. I have lots of work to put in. I have goals." "Amen, brother. Amen. Don't stop until you reach your goal." I nodded again. "I won't."

He asked me how much weight I had lost. I told him I had lost fifty-eight pounds so far. "What's your goal?" "One hundred pounds," I answered. "You can do it!" I gave him the thumbs up sign and increased the volume of my headphones.

An amazing thing happened after that. I hit the play button on my phone, and the same song that was playing when I stopped my workout started from the same spot instead of starting from the beginning. That reminded me that I was like the playlist. I did not stop; I just hit the pause button for a few minutes. My treadmill buddy was absolutely right. I could do it. More importantly, I was going to do it. My why would not let me stop until I accomplished my goal.

Chapter Eleven

Ripples of Success

The harder the conflict, the more glorious the triumph.
- Thomas Paine

No matter how I tried, sleep escaped me that night. In less than twenty-four hours, I would run in my first 5k race. For years, I talked about registering for a 5k but, to be honest, I had no intention of following through because I knew I couldn't do it. However, somewhere along the way, as I began to reach goals and hit milestones, I began to believe that anything was possible.

Running was definitely not my forte. I still remembered quite vividly the sinking feeling in the pit of my stomach when I arrived at PE class and found out we were running a mile. I would be out of breath before making it half way around the track on the first lap. The slow jog would turn into a brisk walk before finally settling into a slow stroll. I'd watch person after person run past me on the track and know that 1 would be the last person to finish. In fact, the majority of my classmates had finished the mile and were back in the gym while I was still working on finishing those dreaded four laps.

It was only a few days earlier, as I was leaving the gym one morning, that the teal and purple pamphlet caught my eye. Its design had its intended effect, and it was soon in my hand. I read three words and knew immediately I needed to sign up for this race. I had to prove to myself that I could do this. I had talked about running a race for way too long without acting on it.

It was then that I heard a small voice in my head say, "At some point, you have to stop talking and start doing, Antuan." With those words still ringing in my ear, I quickly filled out the registration form and submitted my payment before I could change my mind.

The race was in May and it was only February, so there was plenty of time to get ready. Truth be told, there was also plenty of time to back out. I had to laugh as I walked out of the gym that morning.

I shook my head and said, "You're crazy! You're really going to do this." I immediately told my wife what I had committed myself to do. I needed someone to hold me accountable and ensure I followed through with this race. And so, I found a training program, but for some reason, the idea of distance running scared me and I postponed getting started. My mind constantly brought up those memories of P.E. class, but I knew I needed to begin training. I knew that the only way to cure my fear was to take action, and I took that first step and began training.

Before long, I was able to run two miles without stopping. I knew if I could run two miles, I could run three, and by the end of the program, I could! At that point, I almost decided to not to run the race – after all, I had already proven to myself that I could accomplish anything I put my mind to. But then I remembered those who were counting on me to run, and with that knowledge in mind, I knew I would be at the starting line in May.

After weeks of morning runs and evening resistance training, the moment finally arrived. There were two goals for this race. The first was to run the entire three miles. The second was to not finish last.

I had already run the course a few times to prepare myself for the actual race. My outfit was picked out weeks in advance. My music playlist was set, the songs carefully ordered to provide a boost when I needed it most; 55 minutes of music to help me get through the race. The night before the big day, sleep eventually found me and before I knew it, the morning sun peeked through the curtains and woke me from my slumber.

I ate a light breakfast and went through my checklist to ensure I had everything I needed. Ear phones, race number, towel, warm-up shirt (hey, I needed to look good!), knee brace and heart rate monitor were all in my bag. I was good to go. My wife, daughter, and brother accompanied me to the race.

As my brother helped pin the number on my shirt, my nerves tried to get the best of me, but I assured myself I would be fine. I gave hugs to my loved ones and waved to my cheering section, then made my way through the sea of runners to the starting line.

"I'm really doing this!" I thought to myself. "How crazy is this?" I shook my head and smiled to myself. "You got this, man." A voice counted down from ten. There were so many runners that I was unable to see who it was. Once the voice reached "one," the starter gun sounded. Its echoes bounced from the cars to the buildings and finally filled the clear blue sky. Just like that, the sea of humanity gathered at the starting line began moving. There were faster runners sprinting past me, which was fine. My goal was to simply finish, and not finish last. There I was, running oblivious to others around me. It didn't matter that I was being passed.

I found my pace and passed the first mile marker feeling great. Music was blasting in my ears as I rounded the corner and saw the hill that would lead to the second mile marker. Honestly, by this point, I had already talked myself out of slowing to a walk twice.

As I trudged up the hill with burning lungs and stinging sweat filling my eyes, I saw a little boy up ahead. I squinted through the salty sweat and started looking for ways to maneuver around him. As the distance between us decreased, I saw that this little boy was having a difficult time. He was walking with his head down, his mom urging him to continue. But he was having no part of it. For whatever reason, our eyes met.

Up until then, I had not yet uttered one word to anyone on the course. I was too focused on myself and my goals, and was determined to let nothing stand in my way. But before I realized it, my pace slowed to a walk. With the earphones removed for the first time since starting the race, I introduced myself to the little boy.

"I'm Antuan. What's your name?" He looked up at me with his hair disheveled and sweat and discouragement dripping from his face. Softly he said, "I'm Matthew." I asked him if he was okay. He just looked at me. "How old are you?" I asked. "Eight." he said.

I told him I was new to the area and needed a friend to help me finish the race. I asked him if he'd help me finish, and he agreed. I then asked his mom if it would be okay if Matthew and I finished the race together.

Once she gave her approval, we gave each other a fist bump and started off on the last mile. We ran it slowly, at his pace. We walked when he needed to walk. At this point, my goals were a distant memory. For one mile, Matthew and I talked, jogged, encouraged each other, and vowed to finish the race together. We completed the course and crossed the finish line together. When it was over, he looked up at me and said, "We did it!"

I replied, "We sure did buddy. We sure did." There at the finish line I realized that my success was intertwined with the success of others. Matthew was a great example of that. Had I not decided to take control of my health, our paths would not have crossed and I wouldn't have seen the big smile on his face as we completed our 5K. Because I stayed in the fight, I had my serendipitous encounter with a new young friend and was able to help him achieve victory as well. Not only did my success help others, but the success of others helped me.

This was also the case with a group of special people who followed the blog I created. Like me, they were overcoming obstacles and improving their lives. Each week they integrated my posts of vulnerability and transparency into their curriculum. They saw my struggles and realized that they weren't alone in life and that we all face problems.

All of these experiences caused me to reflect. What if I had not chosen to get healthier? What if I had given up when things became hard? What if I stopped the weeks I gained weight? What if I listened to the voice that said it was okay to stop? I couldn't quit now even if I wanted to because I truly understood the phrase, "You have to realize *who* wins when *you* win!"

I carried that experience in my heart and drew on its strength when I found myself weak. I remembered the ripples of success I had experienced. As a child, I would drop pebbles or rocks in puddles of water and watch how far the ripples went, and I noticed something very interesting about them. When I softly tossed a rock in the water, the ripples would travel only a short distance. Yet, when I threw the rock in the water with more force, the waves traveled much further.

That relationship summed up my experience with Matthew and the group of kids who followed my blog. Because my rock carried the weight of past attempts, fear, guilt, inner strength, resolve, and a host of other things, it was very heavy. That heaviness created a great force because of the sheer number of things I had to overcome. And it was that great force which created waves that reached far and wide.

I once heard that greater struggles bring greater victory. I never fully understood that concept until I began my weight loss journey. When I would think about it, I would always equate my great struggle with my own success. But I realized that view was somewhat short-sighted. The greatness of my victory had to do more with how many people it affected, and not just myself. From that race day forward, I thought about struggle and victory quite differently. Now, because of Matthew and the special group of friends who read my blog, I knew the reason for the greatness of the victory was less about me and more about those who experienced the waves of my victory as well.

After that race, Matthew sought me out and gave me a banana and a small bottle of water. He told me it was his second 5k race. I responded, "Whoa, you're amazing, buddy! This is my first one. I hope to run as well as you one day!"

The smile on his face as he ran off was priceless. That moment and that beaming smile were worth far more than any goal I set to accomplish for myself with my first 5K. I ran a few more races after that and looked for Matthew in the crowd. I hope our paths cross again one day.

Chapter Twelve

The Pursuit

What you get by achieving your goals is not near as important as what you become by achieving your goals.
- Zig Ziglar

My eyes remained fixed on the scale. I could not stop looking at those three numbers. It had to be inaccurate. I gathered my composure and stepped off the scale. Thoughts of what if circled around in my head as I waited for the scale to reset. "What if it was right? What if it really was right?"

Those were the questions that swirled around repeatedly in my head. I wanted it to be right, but I had my doubts. Scales weren't always right. After exhaling, I slowly returned to the platform. Careful not to move, I took every precaution to remain still. My eyes were fixed straight ahead. I feared any sudden or slight movement would cause an inaccurate reading.

After a moment or two, I looked down. The same three numbers were displayed on the scale. Once again, I doubted them and repeated my previous routine again. I stepped off the scale, repeated the same questions in my head, and stepped once more on the scale. The third time had to be the charm. The same results occurred. I wanted to go through the routine a fourth time but I knew there was no need.

335.2

A little over three pounds separated me from my goal of losing one hundred pounds. Excitement, disbelief, more excitement, and more disbelief were my companions in that moment. I exhaled a huge sigh of relief.

I had traveled so far to get to this point and, to be honest, I was overwhelmed by it all. I could feel my eyes begin to fill with tears not of sadness, but of joy and relief. The only thing now separating me and my goal was me.

I took a long look in the mirror. For a moment, I did not recognize the man returning my gaze. His features were more chiseled. His countenance was more youthful. I looked through his eyes and saw an intensity and fierceness inside him. The man in the mirror looked as if he could overcome any obstacle in his way. That was a far cry from where he started months ago. The guy in the mirror looked squarely at me and did not say one word. There was no need. His eyes told me everything he wanted to say.

"You got this, Antuan. Three pounds is nothing. Look at what you have already lost." He was not talking about pounds. Along the way, I lost excuses and discarded procrastination. Doubt vanished and his close relative despair followed his lead.

Fear and countless other iron chains that held me captive were shed as I marched toward my goal. I nodded my head at the guy in the mirror and said, "I'll see you next week." And so it began- The last push to lose my hundredth pound.

There were a few quotes I repeated to myself almost daily. One that came to mind as I walked out of my bathroom that day was, "As soon as you make a decision, you'll be tested to see if you were really serious about the decision you just made." That statement had proven itself true over and over again on my journey. And this time was no different. I looked at the calendar to see the date for my next weigh-in; a few days after my birthday, on a weekend where a great celebration was being planned.

That juxtaposition provided quite the conundrum, for celebrations and weight loss rarely go together. What would I do? How would I handle it? Honestly, the first thought was to postpone the weigh-in a week. That option was very appealing, and the man in the darkened room just months earlier would have taken it. However, he was not the same person that had just returned my stare in the mirror. This new person was going to meet this challenge head on.

Creating solutions had become the norm for me. When I was not able to control the impulse to buy chocolate chip cookies at work, I created a solution. Instead of succumbing to the impulses, I carried exact change for a salad. When I wanted to hit the snooze button and stay in bed on those cold Carolina mornings, I made sure my phone was across the room so I would have to get out of the bed when the alarm sounded.

So this latest obstacle (or opportunity) would be met head on. My birthday trip was two days away and would interrupt my routine, so I wouldn't have seven days to completely focus on my goal. In fact, the trip would leave just a handful of days for me to be "all in." During those days, every decision would have to be the best decision I could make. There was no room for shortened sets in the gym, no room for junk calories. Those days had to be days of perfection that would allow me the opportunity to relax a little and enjoy my birthday celebration.

I had my plan and was ready to execute. It was not guaranteed to work, but if it didn't, it wouldn't be from a lack of effort on my part. When the morning of my weigh-in arrived, I woke up at my normal time. Actually, my eyes opened a few minutes before the alarm sounded. Without hesitation, I got up and immediately prepared for my last workout. The ride to the gym was a little shorter this morning, as excitement and nervousness accompanied me.

That morning, dumbbells were lifted, meters were rowed, and miles were run. There was a focus and intensity that I had not experienced before. By the end of my workout, every muscle was on fire and the pools of sweat were doing nothing to quench it.

As I walked back to the car, I was not sure if those handful of days would be enough to meet my goal. In hindsight, I saw places where more could have been done. But it was too late for the would've, could've, and should've. Within twenty minutes, I would know if the goal set during one of the lowest points of my life would be reached.

While I drove home, I found myself lost in my thoughts. The radio was on but had become merely a dull hum in the background. Trees bursting with vibrate orange and red leaves announcing the arrival of fall raced by me unnoticed as I drove down the road.

"What if I didn't lose three pounds this week?" I asked myself. That was a very real possibility but I was completely at peace with it. The previous weekend would have been deemed a complete failure if I were following a diet. For my birthday, I had enjoyed a delectable meal complete with appetizers and an entrée prepared and served in a creamy sauce. Besides the time spent with people I cherished the most, the most amazing part was I enjoyed the meal free from guilt. The past few months taught me that two "bad" days would not derail a healthy lifestyle.

I arrived at my house with a peace and tranquility that would transcend the scale, because I knew I was winning. My mindset had changed, and those changes had leaked into other parts of my life. The same principles I discovered in becoming a healthier version of me lent themselves very well to accomplishing other goals I set. A brand new Antuan was precisely what I had become. I was healthier, stronger, and happier.

When I first started down the path to weight loss, I didn't know if I could lose a hundred pounds, to be honest. However, I did know that I could lose one pound. In my mind, if I could lose one pound, I could do the same thing a hundred times. It was with that mindset that I exited the car and headed into the house. If I did not lose the three pounds this week, it was okay. I knew how to lose one pound and could repeat that three times.

My cell phone rang as I walked through the door. It was my dad asking if I had weighed in yet. Immediately after we hung up, a mist of nervousness slowly crept into my mind. I wanted to make that man proud. He was my father and I loved the fact he was proud of me.

The nervousness quickly evaporated when I saw my wife. "Did you weigh in yet?" she asked. "Not yet, just made it upstairs." I responded.

"Daddy? Did you do it?" asked a certain eleven-year-old girl. "I don't know yet, Champ. I haven't weighed." "What are you waiting on? You scared?" she inquired. "A little," I said in a moment of complete transparency. "Aww, don't be scared," she answered. "Remember what you told me when I didn't want to put my face in the water during swimming lessons and when I was scared to try a round-off back handspring?"

I smiled and said, "I do." "Well, let me hear you say it." I responded without thinking, "I'm a winner and a champion and I can do all things through Christ who strengthens me." "Say it again!" She commanded.

I repeated it, but this time with more conviction. That young girl, wise beyond her years, gave me a high five and ran from the room. "Here we go, Antuan."

Those were the words I spoke softly to myself as I made my way to the scale. I looked up and saw the man in the mirror from the previous week. I nodded at him as he nodded at me. I took a deep breath and stepped on the scale. My eyes were closed as I stood there traversing the memories of the past few years. Both the good and the not so good memories flooded my mind in that moment, and I realized all of them were needed to get me to this point, as my journey of discovery and perseverance would not be possible without them.

I exhaled, opened my eyes and let them travel down to the display, and I had to laugh. I stood on the scale so long that it turned off. I shook my head and stepped off and took a moment to ensure the scale reset before stepping on once again.

This time I found the display screen. The E-R-R from my first weigh-in was now a distant memory, and in its place were four numbers.

331.8.

I did it!

I had lost almost three and a half pounds the previous week. More importantly, I stood on that scale one hundred pounds lighter! The yell that came from deep within me signaled to my wife and daughter that I accomplished my goal. When I came out of the bathroom they both tackled me with hugs and congratulations. The sadness and despair that fueled my tears in that dark room months ago were gone to be replaced by ones made of joy, gratefulness, and exuberance.

To say I was elated was a complete understatement. The feeling I had was indescribable. I completely understood the emotion Will Smith's character was experiencing in the last scene of *The Pursuit of Happyness.*

All I could say was I did it! I actually did it! I sat on the bed and just looked around the bedroom. That moment was a microcosm of the past few months of my life. I was sitting on the same bed, looking at the same furniture, and yet I was in a different house. Along the way, I sold the house where I started my journey and relocated. However, there was a sense of a familiarity in my new environment. The more things appeared to be different the more I realized they were the same. The furniture in my bedroom reminded me of that.

As I thought about this, it occurred to me that this was a great analogy for my own passage to better health. My initial physical condition was also gone. I was now living a healthy lifestyle and going through life with a new mindset, yet the same dreams and aspirations I had when I started were still there. I walked out of the room that morning, and everything was different. The darkness was now light. The despair was now a hope for a great future. The sadness was replaced with joy.

As I walked out of the room, I saw the guy in the mirror one more time. We nodded at each other and I simply asked, "What next?" I stood at the bedroom door briefly looking in the mirror. I answered both myself and the new man in the mirror.

"Whatever you want. It's a brand new Antuan."

Epilogue

To be perfectly clear, I am no superhero. I am simply a person who refused to quit. I had ordinary skill but phenomenal will. My story is not unlike countless others who have succeeded at weight loss. During my journey, there was one question I was asked often. "What's your secret?"

Initially, my response was that there is no secret. As my journey unfolded, I realized there actually was a secret, and that I had found it. It was not a pill that melted belly fat or made my legs smaller. Nor was it a specially formulated juice. The secret was not sold in stores for $19.99, so there was no need to act now or hurry before the offer expired. As a matter of fact, the secret to my weight loss was not found in stores or extracted from an exotic flower in the rainforest.

The true secret to weight loss was extremely powerful. It allowed me to change my life and the lives of others. By having the secret I was able to overcome the obstacles placed in my path as I marched toward my goal. When properly used, the secret led to success in other areas of my life. The best part of the secret was the lack of side effects. There was no list of things that could happen because of it. There was no drowsiness, sickness, headaches, blurred vision, stuffy nose, or watery eyes. I was so confident in the secret and its ability to help me lose weight that I would personally refund someone's money if they were not satisfied with their own results in applying it to their lives.

As these words are read, you're probably saying, "Just tell me already! What's the secret?!?"

So anxious to know what it is, you're getting slightly upset that I'm dragging this out. For those who want to know the secret, I'll tell you and I'll even tell you where to get it.

If you're sitting down, I need you to stand to your feet. Once standing, make your way to the nearest mirror. Close your eyes. Open them. Look deeply in the mirror. Take a deep breath and realize that what you see in the mirror is the secret to weight loss. To be honest, you can replace weight loss with any goal you wish to achieve. My goal happened to be health-related. Weight loss may not be the thing you want to achieve. Whatever your goal, dream or desire is, there is one thing you need to know. Everything needed to accomplish it is already in your possession.

For me, the trials and challenges I encountered allowed me the opportunity to discover and cultivate the seeds of greatness within. Had it not been for adversity, I doubt I would have found the drive, commitment, and perseverance to lose a hundred pounds. There are no gimmicks or shortcuts to success. When you find yourself and adversity staring each other eye to eye, please remember you are the secret. Your success is completely up to you. That's the real key to your success.

Take full advantage of the secret. I am.